RUNNING TO WIN!

Idea-rich Strategies for Leadership and Career Success

Bob 'Idea Man' Hooey
Author of Running TOO Fast

ISBN: 9798675117369 *3rd edition - Updated 2020*

Take Time

Take time to think…
It is the source of power.
Take time to play…
It is the secret of perpetual youth.
Take time to read…
It is the fountain of wisdom.
Take time to pray…
It is the greatest power on earth.
Take time to love and be loved…
It is a God given privilege.
Take time to be friendly…
It is the road to happiness.
Take time to laugh…
It is the music of the soul.
Take time to give…
It is too short a day to be selfish.
Take time to work…
It is the price of success.
Take time to do charity…
It is the key to heaven.

Anonymous

Running to WIN!
Idea-rich strategies for timely leadership and career success

Several years back I was driving home to Calgary from Lethbridge, AB early one winter morning. I had been working with Southern Alberta clients all week and wanted to get back to the office early so I could drop off my paperwork, get a bit of catch up done, and start my weekend. I was making good time cruising down the highway with the radio playing some great tunes. Then, I noticed a sign saying Castlegar, BC only 65 miles. Whoa! I pulled over and collected my thoughts.

How could that be? I was heading home to Calgary, Alberta! Somehow in my overworked, tired brain I had driven right through Fort Macleod and missed at least two BIG highway signs reminding me to turn 'RIGHT', to head 'NORTH' to Calgary. Sure, I was making great time, but I was going in the 'wrong' direction.

We live in an increasingly hectic and demanding world. The demands of running a business or having a successful career overlap and conflict with the demands of having a life, being a spouse or parent, and enjoying the fruits of our labor. Many of us are already running as fast as we can – perhaps Running TOO Fast, and we're not keeping up.

- Many of us are running without knowing where the finish line is located.
- We are running without a real sense of purpose and we are running alone.
- This is a recipe for failure and frustration.

You can finish your race and still have a life!

This revised mini-book (2020) is designed for those who are **'Running to WIN!'** It is written by someone who has learned the value of leveraging his time investment for greater success and productivity, the hard way. ☺ You can too!

Bob 'Idea Man' Hooey, *Author of "Running TOO Fast" and "Think Beyond the FIRST Sale"*

"It's not always that we need to do more but rather that we need to focus on less."
Nathan W. Morris

Table of contents

Check out **Running TOO Fast** for more in-depth analysis and ideas.

Available on

https://www.smashwords.com/profile/view/Hooey and www.SuccessPublications.ca

Chapter 1: Running to WIN! – *Idea-rich strategies for timely leadership and career success*

If you are like me, you may occasionally find yourself with too much on your already **'full'** plate. You've said **'YES'** a few too many times, without counting the cost, or estimating the time needed to do what you've just promised on the run. As a prolific writer and globe trotting speaker I am constantly tempted to take on 'just one more client', 'just one more engagement', or 'just one more writing project.' In doing so, I often find myself staying up late to meet commitments or rushing from airport to venue. **Run your race and still have a life!**

Sound familiar? Welcome to the overcommitted club! If this is just a momentary or temporary overload, you can dig in and work your way through it; or wait until you can get a handle on the commitments you've made. Then you can relax and get back to a more **normal schedule.**

But, if this is your **'life', then this little book is for you!** I'd suggest a long pause… to reflect and refocus; may be **d*e*s*p*e*r*a*t*e*l*y** in order.

Take hope – take action! You can make the necessary changes to free up your time for the important people and priorities in your life. It can be done, and you can do it! With the death of both my parents in 1999 I invested time to reflect and a chance to review and refocus my life and my career in communication. I also had time to finish a few writing projects while caring for my mom until she passed.

My mom, a former English teacher, was my original proof-reader, and she was amazed I could write like this… When Irene and I got married back in 2008, my priorities and time commitments changed again, for the better.

First, let's clear up the common misnomer of **'time management.'** Time cannot really be managed. We can manage others and ourselves in relation to time, but we cannot manage time itself. It will keep ticking along, slipping through our fingers like the ***sands in an hourglass***, even when we wish it wouldn't.

We can choose to control how and where we spend or invest our time. **Life or SELF-management based on value-based judgements** is what is meant when we use the words 'time management'. The time and life management techniques briefly shared here can easily save you an hour or more each day. The real question is… **'What will you do with those extra hours?'** Where will you invest them? How will you leverage them to more flexibility and success?

'No doubt overcommitted people find help in better time management techniques, but many of them will use their newfound skills to pack more obligations into their lives, rather than step back from their madcap pace.'
Howard Macy

Take a moment… **Decide right NOW where the extra time you decide to free up will be invested. Yes, invested and leveraged!**

- Will your family reap the benefits of your better management of your time?

- Will you spend more effective time building your self-esteem by preparing yourself to meet the challenges of our quickly changing world?

- Will you choose to invest this recaptured time in helping others?

- Will you invest time doing something fun?

It's your time. Why not choose to invest it more wisely? Buying and reading this book is a step in the right direction!

"Just because you have the skills, doesn't mean you have the time."
Bob 'Idea Man' Hooey © 1991

Japanese 23rd Psalm

When stress overwhelms you, the Japanese
version of the 23rd Psalm can be helpful.

The Lord is my Pacesetter, I shall not rush.
He makes me stop for quiet intervals;
He provides me with pictures of stillness,
Which restores my serenity.
He leads me in the way of efficiency through
calmness of mind, His guidance is peace.
Even though I have a great many things to
accomplish each day, I will not fret,
for His presence is with me.
His timelessness, His importance,
will keep me in balance.
He prepares refreshment and renewal in
the midst of any activity by anointing me
with the oil of his tranquility.
My cup of joyous energy overflows.
Surely harmony and effectiveness
shall be the fruit of my hours, and I
shall walk in the pace of the Lord,
and dwell in His house forever.

Author Unknown

Chapter 2: How much is your time 'really' worth?

Have you ever taken a moment to think about what your time is **really** worth? Have you ever calculated your earning capacity on an hourly or on a quarterly (15 min) basis? This can be a great educational exercise in determining your worth, relative value, and earning contribution. It can also tell you how much 'each' hour you allow to be wasted is really costing you.

Let's figure it out together.

Let's take a typical example, assuming 52, 5-day weeks in a year.

We will deduct 2, 5-day weeks for normal vacation time. This leaves us 250 days. If you have more vacation time… factor that number in here.

Then, deduct the holidays. In Canada we have 10-12 per year, so let's take 10 on average

This will leave us with only 240 workdays in which to earn our salary or money.

Assuming an average 8-hour workday this gives us **1920 'potential' work hours in a year.**

On the surface, we'd simply take our Gross Pay and divide by the hours, e.g. $50,000/year would give us an average hourly rate of $26.04 per hour. So, in this instance each 15-minute block of recaptured or **wasted time would be costing you $6.51.**

Let's take this a bit further, shall we? In all honesty,
would you say that you are able to get a **'full'** 8
'productive' hours in each 8-hour day? Me either! ☺
Even when I am disciplined, I still have distractions.

If you are in sales, how much of your time is spent selling
or servicing your clients? If you are in leadership, how
much of your time is spent working with your team?

My contention, based on feedback from thousands of
our North American audience members, is the 'true
productivity number' is somewhere closer **to 60%
effectiveness on any given day.** Perhaps, in some
instances, that is optimistic. Let's go with that for this
exercise. If that is true, then we really have only **1152
work hours** in which to make our money.

In the previous example, each hour would now be worth
$43.04 and each 15-minute block would cost us $10.85.

I'll give you some rough comparisons for different dollar
levels.

Annual Earnings	Hourly rate	60% Effective rate	15 min. block
50,000/year	$26.04	$43.40	$10.85
100,000/year	$52.08	$86.80	$21.70
200,000/year	$104.16	$173.60	$43.40

Very interesting numbers, aren't they? If you are
aware of what your time is 'really' worth it will help you
keep an eye on the time wasters that creep into your life.
Not that I put a monetary price on everything in my life;
but it is good to know what my 'investment' is worth.

Mom and Dad at their 50th anniversary

After my dad died in 1999, I spent quite a lot of time with my mom before she passed, a short 6 months later. It was probably the best return for my investment I've every made - priceless!

I'd do it again, in a heartbeat, if I could. *I would give anything to spend just a little bit of time with either of them. That, to me is the true value of time!*

"As you start to slow down, to cut back on your work hours, and to free yourself from some of your commitments, you're going to have some time on your hands. You may feel the need to start nourishing your body by catching up on your sleep, cleaning up your eating patterns, restoring your energy, re-establishing an exercise regimen, spending some time in nature, and learning how to laugh and have fun."
Elaine St. James

Chapter 3: Identifying and eliminating your time wasters

Over the years, we've asked our audiences about their time challenges, and have been able to identify the **25 most common, biggest time wasters.**

Our audiences across the globe have helped us come up with some novel approaches to help combat them.

Here they are!

Telephone interruptions

Failure to plan

Attempting TOO much

Drop-in Visitors

Socializing (can now include social media) and

daydreaming

Ineffective or non-existent delegation

Travel (commuting)

Lack of self-discipline

Inability to say NO!

Procrastination or making 'busy' work

Family concerns

Paperwork - *where is the paperless office they promised us?*

Leaving tasks unfinished

Not enough staff or personnel

Meetings *(unnecessary or unproductive)*

Confused responsibility - *I thought you were going to do that?*

Poor verbal and written communication skills

Inadequate controls, feedback, or progress reports

Inaccurate information

Personal and corporate disorganization

Faxes and email *(great if targeted and used appropriately)*

Management by CRISIS!

Cell phones (they can be great if used properly)

Television

Surfing the Internet and social media (ok…I get caught up in it too!) www.ideaman.net

You may have some of your own time wasters, not on this list. Take a moment to honestly appraise your life and activities.

Go through this list. Check off the time wasters you recognize, *(and remember the people who employ them against you)*, that are draining your schedule and energy.

Once you've identified the major ones, decide to work on each one until you've mastered it.

Successful life and time management is a journey **not** a destination. As in any journey, the starting point is just as important as the destination. Start where you are with a solid focus of where you want to go. Then go for it!

One tip: Don't try to deal with them all at once. Strategically select a few, and work diligently on them, until you've beaten them or got them under control.

Then confidently tackle the next ones on your list. It may take some time but focus your energies. **You can take control!**

'Luck is only important in so far as getting the chance to sell yourself at the right moment. After that, you've got to have talent and know how to use it' **Frank Sinatra**

Chapter 4: Cherish Today!

'Yesterday is but a dream, tomorrow a vision of hope.

Look to this day, for it is life. I cannot change yesterday.

I can only make the most of today and look with hope toward tomorrow!' Anonymous

Review the list of time wasters covered earlier. Pick your **top five** and put them on this list. Take a few minutes and jot down what you think is the real cause (be brutally honest now) and discuss possible solutions with your friends and colleagues. Then set a start time and date when you **'WILL' put your best choice, strategy, or solution into practice.**

As you discuss some of these time wasters, new ideas may pop into your mind. Write them down and share them with your friends.

Brainstorm real solutions to real problems... then commit immediately to put those ideas into action!

Time Waster:

Root Cause:

Potential Solutions:

Start working to fix it:

Completion:

Harness the power of your schedule

Successful people create routines and schedules that allow them to focus their energies on the most important activities needed. They know the value of applied habit and routine as proven by champions in every field. They work to streamline their schedules and minimize those activities that distract them. They plan for success and build strong systematic success habits.

Prioritize one item per day. Focus on your highest value or one of your vital few activities that moves you forward.

Use a 'Focused Five' approach as you plan your work week.

Schedule email and return phone calls. Group them.

No meetings unless they are decisive. Guard your time!

Set a daily routine. Build success habits that allow you to win.

Manage the mornings. Do your vital few activities first thing.

Do something easy first – to kick start your day. Success to start.

Never schedule more than 50% of your day. Life happens despite our schedule, so plan for it.

Design in flex-time to allow for 'interruptions'.
Schedule more time than you think something will take.
I'd suggest scheduling 125% as a rule.

Chapter 5: P*R*I*O*R*I*T*I*E*S

'A hundred years from now it will not matter what size my back account was, the sort of house I lived in, or the kind of car I drove...but the world may be different because I was important in the life of a child.' Anonymous

One helpful suggestion in your life and time management might be in being crystal clear on your priorities in life and business. Remaining focused on the priorities in your personal and family life makes it easier to balance and blend them with the demands of your business, community, and career priorities. Far too many of us have personally paid the price for being unbalanced in our priorities and have lost partners and families. These needless personal tragedies could have been avoided if **we'd only invested the time!**

Someone challenged me, that to be truly effective in my life I should begin to *'schedule my priorities instead of just prioritizing my schedule.'* WOW! This subtle change has made a major difference in its results and the accompanied lifestyle benefits.

Knowing what your priorities are and scheduling specific time each week to work on them brings freedom.

It helps you say 'NO!' to demands and people that don't fall in line or would distract you from seeing your priorities fulfilled.

You are better informed and able evaluate decisions, time investments, resource allotments, and specific goals. You can become more productive when you are working on the important projects in your career. You become more fulfilled when you spend time with the more important people in your life.

I'd suggest spending a few moments on a regular basis revisit and revise your priorities.

PLAN monthly, SCHEDULE weekly, and LIVE daily!

Take a moment and make a note to yourself about these various areas and your changing priorities. Spend time later to refine and focus your thoughts. Keep your written priorities clear, concise, and focused.

Update them regularly. **Ask yourself... what is the SINGLE most important activity I can do this week or today to help me reach my goals in this specific area?**

I've used the following five to help me keep focused over the years

FAMILY:

SELF-IMPROVEMENT:

CAREER:

COMMUNITY:

SPIRITUAL/SPORTS/HOBBIES:

In my case, I routinely schedule my **focused five** activities, as outlined here.

I ask myself the key question in each area and then I write it in my Day-Timer to allocate the time to make it happen. *(Yes, I still use a paper Day-Timer in addition to my electronic reminders. Just writing it down helps anchor it in my memory.)*

I take a careful look at my goals and areas of concern and try to schedule the five most important activities first.

Then I schedule the remainder of my activities. This has made a tremendous difference!

You might want to add a couple more areas or redefine them to help make it more focused for you. I might suggest adding:

WORK/BUSINESS: (separate from career)

PERSONAL: (separate from family and others)

If you've taken the time to fill out this section, I'd like to commend you.

Did you realize that you have now done what 95% of your fellow North Americans never have? Most people have never taken even a few minutes to look at their lives and give some serious thought to their goals and values. **And they wonder why their lives have been less than productive and fulfilling.** Hmmm!

This time of reflection and refocus can be a pivotal point in gaining effective control of your time and life. Please take the time to pause and ponder your priorities. It is worth it!

One bonus tip: **Manage your mornings!** Schedule your most 'important, strategic' activities early in your day before you get distracted by the 'urgent' ones that pop up to sidetrack you.

Chapter 6: Four P's of Personal Performance

Our days will be more effectively used, when we plan or block out our time, based on what I call the **4 P's of Personal Performance.** In brief, here they are:

PEOPLE/PAY DAYS: Our success in life and business is **directly** related to our ability to relate and work with other people. In business, our success is very dependent on maintaining good working relationships with our co-workers, our employees, our employers, our suppliers, our competition, and most importantly our clients or customers.

Simply put, **a people/pay day** is one where the **major** focus is on finding, building, and maintaining the relationships that are important in your life and business profitability. Spending time nurturing and augmenting these relationships can work miracles in team building, customer loyalty, and business longevity.

POWER/PAPERWORK DAY: There are days when the deadlines, the commitments, and the process of running our business and career have to be our **major** focus. And rightly so! The work must be done, the business must be managed, and the bills and orders must be processed.

Power/Paperwork days are the days in which **we set aside blocks of uninterrupted time** to focus on specific projects or obligations and work through to make sure they are completed properly and on schedule.

Days when the work must be about the work – really do WORK!

PAUSE/PLAY DAY: There are days when we need to regenerate, to relax, take a break from our labours, enjoy our families, and sometimes daydream or even goof-off. Days, in which we have fun, not focused on building a business, or in pursuit of training that will advance our careers. Don't forget to schedule these, as they are critical.

Maybe we take a **'fun'** course in something unrelated to what we do - just for the **joy of learning.** Maybe we take part of an afternoon off and sit quietly on a swing, or at the beach, watching the clouds as they slowly meander across the sky.

Pause/Play days allow us to reflect and refocus our energies, priorities, and resources; and **make life worthwhile!** They are most effective in helping us regain control and in balancing our power and people days to maximize our effectiveness. They are critical components to a more balanced, flexible, and successful life!

PLANNING/PREP DAY: These are days allocated, weekly, monthly or quarterly, to plan and work 'on' the business, not 'in' the business; days when the focus is on strategic planning, analysis, and other functions of a long-range perspective.

People spend and excessive amount of time conjugating three verbs: **To Want, To Have, To Do.** *We had forgotten that* **'To Be'** *is the source and fount of life.   Unknown*

I designed specific places for certain information and resources I use regularly for each of my various career, business, and personal involvements. I have a flexible system (still under refinement) for finding the remainder, when needed. This has become even more important as my writing and speaking commitments increased.

As my communications, publishing, and consulting business expands, the plan is to contract out some parts to have the office and accounting work done. This will free me to do what I do and love best!

I re-designed my work area with a large full-sized U-shaped desk to accommodate my changing needs. It allows me to creatively work on several different projects in the same time frame, without excess clutter. Lately with Zoom calls and training from the office, I have needed to make sure it is clear of clutter when filming.

I cut back on my 'collecting' and am working harder at only handling paper once. I have even taken to opening my mail 'over' a wastebasket. This has made some major changes in reducing my bulging filing cabinets and in seeing my desk surfaces.

(2020) When we were organizing our on-line Speakers roundtable for Barcelona, I had one speaker say, "Do you have a new office?" My response, "No, I just cleaned up the clutter."

A friend told me, *"Each piece of paper on my desk was a decision I hadn't made yet."* Ouch, that one got to me! I have even started periodically purging my files of duplicate material, carbon-dated files ☺, and other areas that I used to think *"I had to keep that one on file". Still a way to go but I am getting it under control.*

Take heart, if you find yourself fighting a few uphill battles to regain control of your time and life. It can be done, but it will require you to concentrate and focus your efforts.

As someone once said, *"Inch by inch...life's a pinch, but yard by yard... life can be hard!"* Keep at it - you are **definitely** worth it! Your family and friends will thank you for the hard work. **Keep focused on your goal and keep running to win!**

Chapter 7: Converting Filler Time to Foundation Time

One of the secrets to regaining control of your time and life is in the strategic conversion of 'filler' or wasted time into 'foundation' or constructive time. Recapturing those seemingly *'insignificant'* slices of time (5 to 15-minute chunks) and converting them to constructive use will make a major difference in your life, career advancement, and long- term business or leadership success.

What I'd suggest here are ideas that might help you do just that - capture those 'insignificant' minutes and convert them to useful time.

Useful time, that builds a foundation for success under your dreams and goals.

Useful time, that leads you productively in the direction you've laid out for your future.

Useful time, that previously was wasted or thrown away.

Feel free to add your own suggestions. If you have some new or unique ideas, I'd love to hear them and will include them in subsequent editions of this work. bhooey@mcsnet.ca

At home…

Bunch or group your errands and activities.

Spend 5-10 minutes each day planning your schedule and activities.

Trade off with neighbours or friends and share common chores - i.e., kids to school.

Use your time in the shower as planning time to mentally go over your daily schedule.

Coordinate and lay out your business clothing before you go to bed.

Coordinate your business clothing to include suits, shirts, ties, accessories, etc. Or, blouses, skirts, jackets, etc. Never make more than one trip, if possible. Don't backtrack! Plan a progressive route.

Use a voice mail system on your home phone. Some systems can assign voice mailboxes for each family member. Note: With the advent of cell phones, this may not be as valid.

Open your mail over a recycling bin. Perhaps have one close to the door so you can trash as you sort.
Limit your TV time and watch what brings value or enjoyment to you.

Read something that enriches your life, inspires your soul, or adds value to your career or business.

Limit your internet time checking social media or playing on-line games. This has evolved into a major black 'time sucking' hole for many people in our audiences.

Multi-task to combine activities that would normally demand down time or waiting time, for example, cooking and laundry or menu planning.

Agree on a special family times to discuss and plan family activities.

Other ideas that may come to mind:

At work…

Spend 5-10 minutes each day reviewing the current day and planning activities and goals for the next day. Revise your schedule based on 4 P's of Personal Performance principles. (People/Pay days; Power/Paperwork day; Pause/Play day; and Planning/Prep day.) *Perhaps even do this at the end of your day to plan for tomorrow.*

Keep a folder with required reading close at hand for those 'on-hold' fun times.

Keep a career enhancement book (print, eBook, or reader format) close at hand for creative reading breaks.

Open your business mail over your wastebasket.
Batch your phone calls for specific times each day.

Where feasible, return phone calls at specific times each day.

Where feasible, return your emails at specific times each day.

Minimize your time on Facebook, LinkedIn, and YouTube while at work, or working on a time sensitive project.

Unless you are doing research, keep your surfing to a minimum.

Plan what you are going to say before you make a call and have the relevant information or files available for quick reference.

Multi-task to do more than one job, alternating back and forth between activities instead of just waiting for something to warm up, print, or load.

Trade off with co-workers to create some 'uninterrupted' planning and creative time.

Other ideas that may come to mind:

While waiting...

Carry a book (e-reader) or something to read with you.

Use your Cell phone to retrieve and return messages.

Have a mini-recorder to dictate letters or brainstorm ideas. Use your phone to record messages or text to yourself.

This might be a good time to check and return emails.

This might also be a great time to tweet, check your Facebook, or other social media accounts.

Other ideas that may come to mind:

While commuting...

Turn your car into a mobile university - listen to MP3s, or DVDs en-route.

If using public systems - use your phone or a personal MP3 player and carphones.
If you are on the phone, make sure you are using a hands-free device. Many areas fine distracted drivers.

Spend the time revising your schedule and revisiting your priorities and goals.

Other ideas that may come to mind:

While traveling…

Pre-select your seat whenever possible. Most airlines will allow you to do this in advance of coming to airport. It is worth the extra cost.

Print your boarding pass ahead of time or download to your Smart Phone.

Pack light to save time checking in and waiting at the luggage carousel.

Carry selected reading to review enroute. I now load my tablet with a mix of business and fiction books.

Take along postcards to send notes and thank you' s to selected friends, clients, suppliers, and other important people in your life.

Take time to review and plan your week in relation to 4 P's of Personal Performance.

Take the time to specifically plan and revise your planning tool.

Review magazines and articles that apply to your field of study.

Other ideas that may come to mind:

-
-
-
-
-

I realize the above are not the 'end all - be all' of how to recapture your time. The exercise here was to show you a few examples of areas where you could reclaim a few minutes here and there to free up time for better or more productive use.

As you become focused on recapturing and reclaiming your time, you'll become aware of a multitude of ideas and activities that you can use to convert your filler time into foundation time.

Don't despise those *'insignificant'* minutes. Just like the 'secret' of compound interest, those minutes if captured and reinvested in your career or future will pay fabulous dividends.

If you come up with some unique or creative ideas, please email me and share them? If included in subsequent versions of this work, we will credit you and send you a copy of the updated version.

'Carpo Momento' - seize the moment!

Bob 'Idea Man' Hooey

Chapter 8: Bob's TIME TRICKS

A few quick tips to help you get more control of your time and make your life more productive.

1.   Use lists (Specific kinds)

Tapping into the power of making lists

Making lists can be one of the most productive or frustrating things you do. Here are some productive lists to add to your already 'overfull **To Do**' one.

BIG Picture list: this is where you can outline all the items you have on your lists, so you can see where they fit.

Stop doing list: actions or activities that you will delete from your agenda; actions that you are committed to stop doing.

Projects list: a collection of all projects on your agenda (big picture of where you are already committed.

Next Action list: with sequential steps or actions on a project.

Waiting for list: parking lot of items you need to move forward or items that others need to do before you can complete yours.

Calendar list: simple dates and deadlines for meetings, activities, projects, and other scheduled activities or commitments.

Someday list: is where you park all those items or activities that you just never seem to have time for…
 if you do have some time open up you can check here and pick one to complete.

Bucket list: might be a good idea for dreams and adventures.

2. In-box strategy

Get to the bottom of it daily!
One item at a time!
Never put something back in!

3. Two-minute rule

Any action item that takes less than 2 minutes
DO IT NOW!

4. Weekly rule

Part of the Plan monthly; Schedule weekly, Live daily process of effective self-management in relation to how you allocate your time.

Bonus reminder or 'nudge'

How about putting items by the door that you need to take with you in the morning? Works when going home as well.

Chapter 9: "I just didn't have enough time!"

Ever said that?

YES ✓

NO ☐

The harsh truth is, *'we have all the time there is!'* Each of us has the 'same' 1440 minutes in our day that were given to Bill Gates, Mother Teresa, or another famous person. What makes the difference is how we allocate and leverage those minutes. And, in how we allow others to use or abuse these minutes for us.

Despite a massive selection of seminars, notebooks, To Do lists, computers, and assorted electronic and paper organizers, we still find ourselves too busy and overwhelmed with commitments, obligations, and deadlines.

As leaders, being too busy to invest in working with, coaching, and leading your team can have drastic consequences for everyone.

We mean well, we really do! We even plan to buckle down and manage or schedule our time more effectively. Unfortunately, our human nature works against us, unless we make a disciplined effort to keep our lives and priorities on track.

The TRUTH – WE (not anyone else) are responsible for the gross mis-management of our time and the amount of time WE allow others to waste. We need to learn to say 'NO' to the distractions and the actions that take us away from what is our most important functions, the best use of our expertise, skills, and energies.

- What are we the **'best'** at?

- Why are we not focusing our energies on that **'priority'**?

We have all the 'reasons' why we didn't use our time more wisely or should we say all the 'excuses'. Sometimes the harsh reality gives us a wake-up call when we miss an important deadline because we procrastinated, overcommitted, or underestimated the time needed to finish a project and ran out of time. Sound familiar?

I've heard it said, *"Someone who lacks the will to say 'NO' will always be at the mercy of the time wasters."* There are always people who will take your time. They will steal it, waste it, poison it, and rob you of the very essence of your life; unless you take control and decide for yourself who gets how much time and for what purpose. Remember it's your time and it's your choice!

Today, you can decide to fight and take back control of your time and life! It takes planning and discipline, but it can be done!

One effective technique learned to help recapture my time and life was to set aside **regular time to 'plan'** future activities. A few minutes spent pre-planning each day, before starting, will save you hours! It is amazing what having a daily focus on the most important priority or critical activity can do to help free-up your time and stop saying yes as much!

Similarly, invest regular time weekly and monthly to layout and 'schedule your priorities' (vs. prioritize your schedule), block out specific times, and allocate resources to reach your personal and professional goals. This will make a profound difference in your leadership, life management, and the results of your time investment. It did for me, both professionally and personally.

Learn to **PLAN Monthly, SCHEDULE Weekly, and Lead Daily!**

Where are you on your personal timeline?

0_________X__________ 10

0 = way far behind 10 = doing very well

Take a moment and give yourself an honest evaluation of how well you are doing in managing yourself in relation to the time you have to lead, live, and create a legacy.

Then ask yourself:

What obstacle(s) stands in your way of moving closer to 10?

What do you have to do or say no to doing to move your productivity and leveraged use of time closer to 10?

When are you going to act?

(excerpt from Running TOO Fast – used with permission)

'You've gotta keep control of your time, and you can't unless you say no. You can't let people set your agenda in life' Warren Buffet

About the author

Bob 'Idea Man' Hooey is a charismatic, confident leader, corporate trainer, inspiring facilitator, Emcee, prolific author, and award-winning motivational keynote speaker on leadership, creativity, success, business innovation, and enhancing team performance.

Using personal stories drawn from rich experience, he challenges his audiences to engage his **Ideas At Work!** – To act on what they hear, with clear, innovative building-blocks and field-proven success techniques to increase their effectiveness.

Bob challenges them to hone specific 'success skills' critical to their personal and professional advancement. Bob outlines real-life, results-based, innovative ideas personally drawn from 29 plus years of rich leadership experience in retail, construction, small business, entrepreneurship, manufacturing, association, consulting, community service, and commercial management.

Bob's conversational, often humorous, professional, and sometimes-provocative style continues to inspire and challenge his audiences across North America. Bob's motivational, innovative, challenging, and practical **Ideas**

At Work! have been successfully applied by thousands of leaders and professionals across the globe.

Bob is a frequent contributor to North American consumer, corporate, association, trade, and on-line publications on leadership, success, employee motivation and training; as well as creativity and innovative problem solving, priority and time management, and effective customer service. He is the inspirational author of 30 plus publications.

Visit: **www.SuccessPublications.ca** for more information.

Retired, award winning kitchen designer, Bob Hooey, CKD-Emeritus was one of only 75 Canadian designers to earn this prestigious certification by the National Kitchen and Bath Association.

In December 2000, Bob was given a special CAPS National Presidential award '…for his energetic contribution to the advancement of CAPS and **his living example of the power of one'** in addition to being elected to the CAPS National Board. He has been recognized by the National Speakers Association and other professional groups for his leadership contributions.

Bob is a co-founder and a past President of the CAPS Vancouver & BC Chapter and served as 2012 President of the CAPS Edmonton Chapter.

He is a member of the NSA-Arizona Chapter and an active leader in the National Speakers Association, a charter member of the Canadian Association of Professional Speakers, PSA-Spain, the VSAI, as well as the Global Speakers Federation (GSF). He retired (December 2013) as a Trustee from the CAPS Foundation.

In 1998, Toastmasters International recognized Bob '…**for his professionalism and outstanding achievements in public speaking'**.

That August in Palm Desert, California Bob became the 48th speaker in the world to be awarded this prestigious professional level honor as an Accredited Speaker. He has been inducted into their Hall of Fame on numerous occasions for his leadership contributions. He served as Region Advisor for Toastmasters International 2018-2019.

Bob has been honoured by the United Nations Association of BC (1993) and received the CANADA 125 award (1992) for his ongoing leadership contributions to the community. In 1998, Bob joined 3 other men to sail a 65-foot gaff rigged schooner from Honolulu, Hawaii to Kobe, Japan, barely surviving a 'baby' typhoon en-route.

In November 2011 Bob was awarded the Spirit of CAPS at their annual convention, becoming the 11th speaker to earn this prestigious CAPS National award. Visit: www.ideaman.net/SoC.htm

Bob pictured here presenting at the AFCP conference in Paris, France

Bob loves to travel and his speaking and writing have allowed him to visit 60 countries so far.
www.havemouthwilltravel.com

Perhaps your organization would like to bring Bob in to share a few ideas (virtually or live) with your leaders and teams around the globe.

Ok, I want your business! 😊 I would love the opportunity to explore how we might work together, and how some of my programs or consulting might be a benefit for you or your team. Visit my web sites for more information on what I bring to the table,
www.ideaman.net or **www.BobHooey.training**

Contact him at: **bhooey@mcsnet.ca**

Acknowledgements, credits, and disclaimers

As with each of my books, a very special dedication of this piece of myself, to the two people who meant the most to me, my folks Ron and Marge Hooey. Sadly, both my parents left this earthly realm in 1999. I still miss our time together and your encouragement and love. I was blessed with the two of you in my life.

To my inspiring wife and professional proof-reader and publications coach, Irene Gaudet, who loves, encourages, and supports me in my quest to continue sharing my **Ideas At Work!** across the world. Thank you seems so inadequate for your timely work in helping make my writing and my client service better! I love the time we spend together!

My thanks to the many people who have encouraged me in my growth as a leader, speaker, and engaging trainer in each area of expertise including 'Running to WIN!'.

To my colleagues and friends in the National Speakers Association (NSA), the Canadian Association of Professional Speakers (CAPS), and the Global Speakers Federation (GSF) who continually challenge me to strive for success and increased excellence.

To my great audiences, leaders, students, coaching clients, and readers across the globe who share their experiences and enjoyment of my work.

Your positive and supportive feedback encourages me to keep working on additional programs and success publications like this updated version. My experience with you creates the foundation for additional real-life experiences I can take from the stage to the page, the classroom to the boardroom.

My thanks to a select few friends for your ongoing support and 'constructive' abuse. You know who you are. ☺

Disclaimer

We have not attempted to cite all the authorities and sources consulted in the preparation of this book. To do so would require much more space than is available. The list would include departments of various governments, libraries, industrial institutions, periodicals, and many individuals. Inspiration was drawn from many sources, including other books by the author; in this updated creation of **'Running to WIN!'**

This mini-book is written and designed to provide information on more effective use of your time, as a life and leadership enhancement guide. It is sold with the 'explicit' understanding that the publisher and/or the author are not engaged in rendering legal, accounting, or other professional services. If legal or other expert assistance is required, the services of a competent professional in your geographic area should be sought.

It is not the purpose of this book to reprint all the information that is otherwise available. Its primary purpose is to complement, amplify, and supplement other books and reference materials already available.

You are encouraged to search out and study all the available material, learn as much as possible, and tailor the information to your individual needs. This will help to enhance your success in being a more effective salesperson, leader or professional.

Every effort has been made to make this book as complete and as accurate as possible within the scope of its focus. However, there may be mistakes, both typographical and in content or attribution. Graphics are royalty free or under license. Care has been taken to trace ownership of copyright material contained in this volume. The publisher will gladly receive information that will allow him to rectify any reference or credit line in subsequent editions. This book should be used only as a general guide and not as the ultimate source of information. Furthermore, this book contains information that is current only up to the date of publication.

The purpose of **'Running to Win!'** is to educate and entertain; perhaps to inform and to inspire. It is certainly to challenge its readers to learn and apply its secrets and tips, to challenge them to enhance their skills and leverage their time to create more productive outcomes.

The author and publisher shall have <u>neither</u> liability nor responsibility to any person or entity with respect to any loss or damage caused, or alleged to have been caused, directly or indirectly, by the information contained in this book.

Bob's Publications

Bob is a prolific author who has been capturing and sharing his wisdom and experience in printed and electronic forms for the past twenty plus years. In addition to the following publications he has written for consumer, corporate, professional associations, trade, and on-line publications.

He has also been engaged to write and assist on publications by other writers and companies.

Leadership, business, and career development series

Running TOO Fast (8th edition 2019)
Legacy of Leadership (3rd edition 2019)
Make ME Feel Special! (6th edition 2019)
Why Didn't I 'THINK' of That? (5th edition 2019)
Speaking for Success! (9th edition 2020)
THINK Beyond the First Sale (3rd edition 2019)
Prepare Yourself to Win! (3rd edition 2017)
The early years… 1998-2009 – A Tip of the Hat collection (2020)
The saga continues… 2010-2019 - A Tip of the Hat collection (2020)

Bob's Mini-book success series

The Courage to Lead! (4th edition 2017)

Creative Conflict (3rd edition 2017)
THINK Before You Ink! (3rd edition 2017)
How to Generate More Sales (4th edition 2017)
Unleash your Business Potential (3rd edition 2017)
Maximize Meetings (2019)
Learn to Listen (2nd edition 2017)
Creativity Counts! (2nd edition 2016)
Create Your Future! (3rd edition 2017)

Bob's Pocket Wisdom series

Pocket Wisdom for Speakers (updated 2019)
Pocket Wisdom for Leaders – Power of One! (2019)

Quick read series (2017-2020) - more in 2020

LEAD! *Idea-rich leadership success strategies*
CREATE! *Idea-rich strategies for enhanced innovation*
TIME! *Idea-rich tips for enhanced performance and productivity*
SERVE! *Idea-rich strategies for enhanced customer service*
SPEAK! *Idea-rich tips and techniques for great presentations*
CREATIVE CONFLICT *Idea-rich leadership for team success*
SUCCEED! *Idea-rich strategies to succeed in business, despite global disruptions (2020)*
WRITE ON! *Idea-rich tips and techniques to bring your book into pixels or print (2020)*
Get to YES! *Idea-rich introductions to subtle art of creative persuasion in sales and negotiation (2020)*
Running to WIN! *Idea-rich strategies for timely leadership and career success (2020)*

Co-authored books created by Bob

Quantum Success – 3 volume series (2006)

In the Company of Leaders (95th anniversary Edition 2019)
Foundational Success (2nd Edition 2013)

Visit: **www.SuccessPublications.ca** for more information

'It is no good getting furious if you get stuck. What I do is keep thinking about the problem but work on something else' **Steven Hawking**

I love to share ideas and look forward to hearing what you think about these. bhooey@mcsnet.ca

Connect with me on:

Facebook: www.facebook.com/bob.hooey

LinkedIn: www.linkedin.com/in/canadianideamanbobhooey

YouTube: www.youtube.com/ideamanbob

Smashwords: www.smashwords.com/profile/view/Hooey

Mail: PO Box 10, Egremont, AB, T0A 0Z0

Thanks for purchasing and reading Running to WIN!

Each time I sit down to write, or in this case to re-write, I am challenged to ensure I deliver something that will be of use-it-now value to my reader.

I ask myself, **'If I was reading this, what would I be looking for?'**

As well as, **'Why is this relevant to me, today?'**

These two questions help to keep me focused, help me to remain clear on my objectives; and they help to remind me to dig into my experiences, stories, examples, and research to provide solid information that will be of benefit and help my readers, when they apply it, succeed. That can be an exciting challenge!

I trust I have done that for you in this updated primer on more effective use of your time and leveraging your activities.

Running to WIN! is my attempt to capture some of the lessons learned over the past 25 plus years and to share them with you.

I'd love to hear from you and read your success stories. If you would be so kind, please drop me a quick email at: bob@ideaman.net

Bob 'Idea Man' Hooey
http://www.ideaman.net
http://www.HaveMouthWillTravel.com

What they say about Bob 'Idea Man' Hooey

As I travel across North America and around the globe, sharing my Ideas At Work!, I am fortunate to get feedback and comments from my audiences and colleagues. These comments come from people who have been touched, challenged, or simply enjoyed themselves in one of my sessions.

I'd love to come and share some ideas with your organization and teams. I am available live or in a virtual format to serve you.

"ve known Bob for several years and follow his activities in business with interest. I originally met Bob when he spoke for a Rotary Leadership Institute and got to know him better when he came to Vladivostok, Russia to speak to our leadership. When you spoke I thought you were one of us because you talked about our challenges just like yours. You could understand the others, which makes you a great speaker!' **Andrey Konyushok**, Rotary International District 2225 Governor 2012-2013, far eastern Russia

'I still get comments from people about your presentation. Only a few speakers have left an impression that lasts that long. You hit a spot with the tourism people.' **Janet Bell**, Yukon Economic Forums

We greatly appreciate the energy and effort you put into researching and adapting your keynote to make it more meaningful to our member councils. Early feedback from our delegates indicates that this year's convention was one of our most successful events yet, and we thank you for your contribution to this success.' **Larry Goodhope**, Executive Director Alberta Association of Municipal Districts and Counties *(retired)*

'Thank you Bob; it is always a pleasure to see a true professional at work. You have made the name 'Speaker' stand out as a truism - someone who encourages people to examine their lives and make adjustments. The personal stories you shared with your audience made such a great impression on everyone. The comments indicated you hit people right where it is important - in their hearts. Each of those in your audience took away a new feeling of personal success and encouragement.' **Sherry Knight**, Dimension Eleven Human Resources and Communications

'Bob is one of those rare individuals who knows how to tackle obstacles in life to reach his dreams. He takes each as a learning experience and stretches for more. His compassion and genuine interest in others make him an exceptional coach.' **Cindy Kindret**, Training Manager, Silk FM Radio

'Without doubt, I have gained immeasurable self-assurance. Bob, your patience and your encouragement has been much appreciated. I strongly recommend your course to anyone looking for self-improvement and professional development.' **Jeannie Mura**, Human Resources Chevron Canada

'I am pleased to recommend Bob 'Idea Man' Hooey to any organization looking for a charismatic, confident speaker and seminar leader. I have seen Bob in action on several occasions, and he is ALWAYS on! Bob has the ability to grab his audience's attention and keep it.

Quite simply, if Bob is involved - your program or seminar is guaranteed to succeed.' **Maurice Laving**, Coordinator Training and Development, London Drugs

'I have found Bob's attention to detail and his ability to fine tune his seminars to match the time frame and needs of the audience to be a valuable asset to our educational Program.' **Patsy Schell**, Executive Director Surrey Chamber of Commerce

'Great seeing you in Cancun and congratulations on a job well done. The seminar was a great success! Your humorous and conversational style was a tremendous asset. It is my sincere hope that we can be associated again at future seminars.' **Donald MacPherson**, Attorney At Law, Phoenix, Arizona

'What a great conference. It was a great pleasure meeting with you at the Ritz Carlton, Cancun and I shall look forward to hopefully welcoming you and your family in Dublin, Ireland someday.' **A. Paul Ryan**, Petronva Corporation, Dublin, Ireland

'Congratulations on the Spirit of CAPS Award. You have worked long and hard on behalf of CAPS …helped many speakers including me and richly deserve this award. Well done my friend.' **Peter Legge**, CSP, Hof, CPAE

'I had the pleasure of hearing and watching Bob Hooey deliver a keynote speech several years ago when he gave a presentation at a Toastmasters International Convention. Bob impressed me greatly with his professionalism, energy, and ability to connect with his audience while giving them value. Dr. **Dilip Abayasekara**, DTM, Accredited Speaker, Past Toastmasters International President

Copyright and License Notes

Running to WIN!
Idea-rich strategies for leadership and career success

Bob 'Idea Man' Hooey, Accredited Speaker, 2011 Spirit of CAPS recipient. Prolific author of 30 plus business, leadership, and career success publications. Author, Think Beyond The FIRST Sale

Unattributed quotations are by Bob 'Idea Man' Hooey

Photos of Bob: Bonnie-Jean McAllister,
www.elantraphotography.com
Dov Friedman, www.photographybyDov.com
Editorial, layout and design: **Irene Gaudet,** Vitrak Creative Services, vitrakcreative.com

Success Publications – a division of Creativity Corner Inc.
Box 10, Egremont, AB T0A 0Z0
www.successpublications.ca
Creative office: +1-780-736-0009

Engage Bob for your leaders and their teams

'I have been so excited working with Bob Hooey, as he has given inspiration and motivation to our leadership team members. Both at the Brick Warehouse – Alberta and here at Art Van Furniture – Michigan; with his years of experience in working with business executives and his humorous and delightful packaging of his material, he makes learning with Bob a real joy. But most importantly, anyone who encounters his material is the better for it.' **Kim Yost**, retired CEO Art Van Furniture, former CEO The Brick

Motivate your teams, your employees, and your leaders to more 'productively' grow and 'profitably' succeed!

Protect your conference investment - leverage your training dollars.

Enhance your professional career and sell more products and services.

Equip and motivate your leaders and their teams to grow and succeed, 'even' in tough times!

Leverage your time to enhance your skills, equip your teams, and better serve your clients.

Leverage your leadership and investment of time to leave a significant legacy!

Call today to engage best-selling author, award winning, inspirational leadership keynote speaker, leaders' success coach, and employee development trainer, Bob 'Idea Man' Hooey and his innovative, audience based, results-focused, Ideas At Work! for your next company, convention, leadership, staff, training, or association event. You'll be glad you did!

Call +1-780-736-0009 to connect with **Bob 'Idea Man' Hooey** today!

Learn more about Bob at: www.ideaman.net or www.BobHooey.training

'Improved productivity means less human sweat, not more' Henry Ford

When you are **Running to WIN!** Make sure you look for ways to enhance your productivity along the way.